SPIRITUAL ADVICE

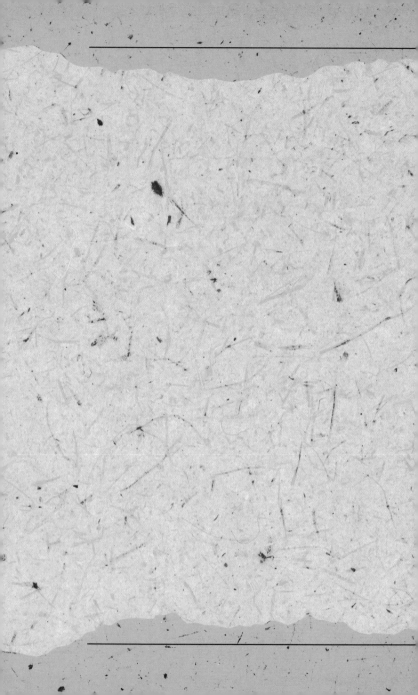

SPIRITUAL ADVICE from

JOHN PAUL II

365 DAYS OF INSPIRATION

Compiled by
Mary Emmanuel Alves, FSP
Molly H. Rosa

Pauline
BOOKS & MEDIA
Boston

Library of Congress Cataloging-in-Publication Data

John Paul II, Pope, 1920–

  [Selections. English. 2003]

  Spiritual Advice from John Paul II / compiled by Mary Emmanuel Alves, Molly H. Rosa.

      p. cm.

  ISBN 0-8198-7070-6

  1. Spiritual life—Catholic Church. 2. Devotional calendars—Catholic Church. 3. Catholic Church—Prayer-books and devotions—English. I. Alves, Mary Emmanuel, 1945– II. Rosa, Molly H. III. Title.

  BX2350.3 J6313 2003

  242'.2—dc21

                       2002015647

Cover photos: © *L'Osservatore Romano* Photo Service

Published in the U.S.A. by Pauline Books & Media, 50 Saint Pauls Avenue, Boston, MA 02130-3491.

Printed in Korea.

www.pauline.org   www.johnpaulpapacy.org

Pauline Books & Media is the publishing house of the Daughters of St. Paul, an international congregation of women religious serving the Church with the communications media.

2 3 4 5 6 7 8 9 10   10 09 08 07 06 05 04

Introduction

Each step along the journey of life brings with it the possibility for new insight, deeper understanding, and greater appreciation for the effort purposeful living requires. However, we can find ourselves struggling to see and to hear what life is telling us, let alone appreciate the hard knocks that are often the watersheds to growth. At moments of difficulty or particular need, we seek out the advice of a trusted friend or persons reputed for wisdom and holiness. But why not benefit from such people every day? In the Old Testament Book of Sirach we read, "If you see a man of understanding, seek him out; let your feet wear away his doorstep!" (6:36)

Pope John Paul II easily stands out as one of the greatest spiritual giants of our times. His compassionate understanding of the human condition and his profound intimacy with God have inspired countless people of every walk of life and faith tradition to listen to and take to heart his wealth of wisdom. The treasure of this collection of his words allows us to walk alongside John Paul as companion pilgrims on the same journey.

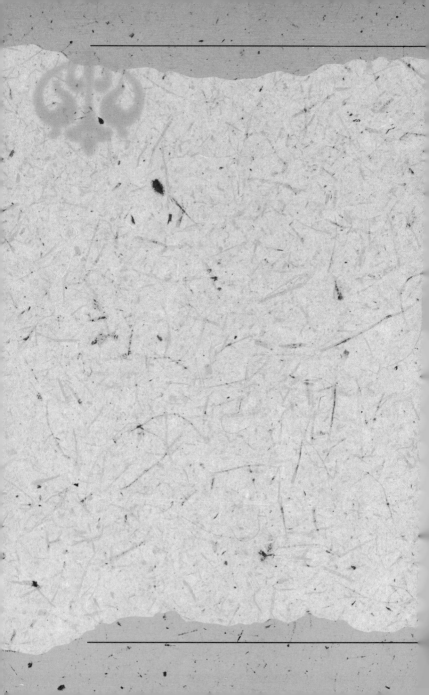

January

$\mathcal{R}$emember that you are never alone; Christ is with you on your journey every day of your lives! He has called you and chosen you to live in the freedom of the children of God. Turn to Christ in prayer and in love. Ask him to grant you the courage and strength to live in this freedom always. Walk with him who is "the Way, the Truth, and the Life"!

January 1

*P*eople today
especially need to rediscover the aspect of
silence and prayer, an indispensable
dimension for opening one's heart to God
and to one's brothers and sisters.

$\mathcal{D}$o not yield to the temptation to regard pain as an experience which is only negative, to the point of doubting God's goodness. In the suffering Christ every sick person finds the meaning of his or her afflictions. Suffering and illness belong to the human condition—we are fragile, limited creatures. In Christ, who died and rose again, however, humanity discovers a new dimension to its suffering: instead of a failure, it reveals itself to be the occasion for offering witness to faith and love.

January 3

January 4

*L*et us pray that every Christian family may be a little missionary church and a school for evangelizers.

$\mathcal{C}$hrist is the true light who has come into the world, the light which "shines in the dark, a light that darkness could not overpower." In fact, only eyes illumined by faith can "see it."

January 5

*I*f God wants to meet us as a human person—indeed, as a child—then we too must reach out to God. We must set out on the road like the shepherds of Bethlehem, like the magi from the East.

You must above all seek peace as harmony and cohesion within your personal, vital structures: interior peace, the fruit of interior struggle, of sincere commitment to a life consistent with your faith, of constant effort to restore persons to the integrity, the harmony, the beauty of their divine origin.... You must "insofar as it be within your power, live in peace with all."

January 7

January 8

Pause before the tabernacle by yourself, for no special reason, even without saying a word, simply remaining in Christ's presence, contemplating the supreme gesture of love contained in the consecrated Bread.

$\mathcal{W}$e must truly give thanks to the Lord, who gives us the opportunity to witness to the Gospel with simplicity, becoming apostles of fidelity and hope on the paths of this world.

January 9

The silence of the mountain and the whiteness of the snow speak to us of God. They show us the way to contemplation, not only as an excellent way to experience the Mystery, but also as a condition for humanizing our life and our mutual relations.

$\mathcal{B}$e faithful to the sublime vocation you have received. Become missionaries by word and example. Nourish your commitment at the wellsprings of Scripture, the sacraments, and the constant praise of God, and let the Spirit's action increasingly penetrate the depths of your soul. You will thus be effective agents of the new evangelization, to which the Church is committed on the threshold of the new millennium.

January 11

January 12

*T*he call for a sincere
gift of self is the fullest way to realize
personal freedom.

The one who renews minds is the Spirit of Truth. Strive to open to the Spirit the interior space of your heart "so that you may judge what is God's will, what is good, pleasing, and perfect" (Rom 12:2).

January 13

Fraternal love leads to the forgiveness of all offenses, does not dispense with human justice, which judges the fault and condemns it. But one advances on the way of peace and reconciliation by first respecting the human person. Without respect it is impossible to rebuild what has been destroyed. This respect of the person is the premise for truly fraternal dialogue.

*B*eing holy means living in deep communion with the God of joy, having a heart free from sin and the sadness of the world, and a mind that is humble before God.

January 15

God's love is a love that awaits with patience and welcomes with rejoicing the person who has been far away; which educates and corrects; which satisfies every person's hunger for love.

*D*on't be so immersed in the work of the Lord that you forget or neglect the Lord of the work.

January 17

January 18

*L*et no one be afraid of the light of Christ! His Gospel is the light, which does not bring death, but which develops and brings to full maturity whatever is true, good, and beautiful in every human culture. The Gospel of Christ is meant for humanity, for the life, peace and freedom of every individual and of all people.

Whoever reflects on the history of the Church with eyes of love will discover that despite the many faults and shadows, there were and still are men and women everywhere whose lives highlight the credibility of the Gospel.

January **19**

January 20

*D*ecide to listen to
Christ and to be imbued with the strength
of divine grace.

*F*ollowing the example of Mary, we must learn to educate the heart to hope, opening it to the "infinite love" of God, who makes us exult with joy and gratitude. For those who respond generously to the Lord's invitation, the happy and sad events of life become the topic for a confidential discussion with the Father. These events become the occasion for unceasing rediscovery of their own identity as beloved children called to participate with a specific and personal role in the great work of the salvation of the world, which was begun by Christ....

January 21

January 22

*P*roclaim and give
witness to the Gospel of life!

*E*verything in the life of the elderly person may serve to fulfill his or her earthly mission. Nothing is in vain. On the contrary, cooperation, precisely because it is hidden, is yet more valuable for the Church.

January 23

*B*y frequently
receiving the sacrament of Reconciliation,
you will discover that Jesus has
confidence in you and loves you without
limits; that the past can be surpassed,
since forgiveness opens up a new future.

*J*esus says to everyone: "Repent and believe in the Gospel" (Mk 1:15). At the origin of every genuine conversion there is God looking upon the sinner. It is a look that becomes a search filled with love; a passion, even that of the cross; a will to pardon that, showing the guilty one the esteem and love in which he or she is still held, in contrast to the disorder in which one is plunged, calls for the decision to change one's way of life.

January 25

January 26

In every part of the earth the Bride of the Lord is called to give thanks to the Father for the mystery of the incarnation of the Son, foundation of unity and victory over every division in the human person and humanity.

I ask you to be "prophets of joy." The world must recognize us by our ability to communicate to our peers the sign of a great hope, which has already been fulfilled: Jesus, who for our sake died and rose again. Do not forget that "the future of humanity is in the hands of those who are capable of providing the generations to come with reasons for life and optimism."

January 27

January 28

*E*verything great
requires patience.

*J*esus is living next to you, in the brothers and sisters with whom you share your daily existence. His visage is that of the poorest, of the marginalized…. Jesus' dwelling is wherever a human person is suffering because rights are denied, hopes betrayed, anxieties ignored. There, in the midst of humankind, is the dwelling of Christ, who asks you to dry every tear in his name, and to remind whoever feels lonely that no one whose hope is placed in Christ is ever alone.

January **29**

The saints are those who in every age know how to courageously live their faith by bearing witness to Christ without surrender or compromise.

$\mathcal{C}$ome to adore the
One who does not forsake those who seek
God with a sincere heart and strive to
keep God's law. Heed God's message,
which strengthens hearts broken and
confused.

January 31

February

*I*n some sense we feel impelled to make our lives a daily offering by showing mercy to our brothers and sisters, drawing upon the gift of God's merciful love. We realize that God, in showing us mercy, calls upon us to become witnesses to mercy in today's world.

February 1

To be with Jesus should be your great desire: to speak with him in a familiar way, to listen to him and follow him docilely. This is not only an understandable demand for whoever wants to follow the Lord, it is also an indispensable condition for all authentic and credible evangelization.

In order to be a
teacher of peace, one must first of all
nurture peace within.

February 3

When Christ says, "Do not be afraid," he wants to respond to the deepest source of the human being's existential fear. He means do not fear evil, since in his resurrection good has shown itself stronger than evil. His Gospel is victorious truth.

$\mathcal{W}$e praise God, the Creator and Lord of the universe, for the gift of life and especially human life, which has blossomed on this planet through the mysterious plan of divine goodness. Life in all its forms is entrusted in a special way to the care of man and woman.

February 5

February 6

*I*n our society of consumerism and images, we easily run the risk of losing ourselves, of ending "in pieces." A shattered mirror can no longer reflect the whole image. It has to be remade. The person thus needs a deep and stable center around which he or she can unify various experiences. This center, as St. Augustine teaches, is not to be sought outside oneself, but deep in one's own heart, where man and woman meet God the Father, the Son, and the Holy Spirit. In the relationship with God who is unity, one can unify oneself.

*M*ake your life a
great song of love and praise!

February 7

February 8

*Y*ou will get to know
God truly and personally only through
prayer. What is needed is that you talk to
God, and listen to God.

$\mathcal{E}$ven though man
and woman are made for each other,
this does not mean that God created
them incomplete. Reciprocity and
complementarity are the two fundamental
characteristics of the human couple.

February 9

February 10

*W*e should
remember...that with health problems
and the decline of our physical strength,
we are particularly associated with Christ
in his passion and on the cross.

$\mathcal{L}$et us look to Mary, the sublime model of the search for truth. Mother of the One who is wisdom itself, her life was a pilgrimage from that one demanding question that opened her to the light of faith. May she help us not to avoid the questions that really matter, those decisive for our life.

February 11

Try then to behave toward Jesus in the Eucharist as he behaves toward us: he gives himself gratuitously.

The Church always has difficulties; many times it is attacked, hindered. But it is always young, always very much alive!

February 13

The salvation offered to us is a gift that should not be jealously hidden. It is like the light of the sun, which by its nature breaks through the darkness. It is like the water of a clear spring, which gushes from the heart of the rock.

Through the parable of the Good Samaritan, Jesus changes the terms of the question [about one's neighbor]. The question is not who is one's neighbor, but rather *who made himself a neighbor* to the poor man who fell victim to the violence of robbers.

February 15

February 16

*Have hope and trust
in God who is ever faithful.*

St. Thérèse of Lisieux commented in her autobiography: "As a lever, God gave the saints prayer that inflames with the fire of love, and this is how they lifted the world" (*Gli scritti*, Rome, 1979, p. 307). Yes, God alone is our true and unfailing support, just as love and prayer are the only sure spiritual levers with which it is possible to lift up the world.

February 17

*B*ring your
questions and fears to the Lord, for in God
you will discover life's true meaning and
your own vocation in this world.

... *A* person who forgives opens the hearts of others and learns to love and understand others by entering into harmony with them. The act of pardoning, after the example of Jesus, challenges and opens hearts, heals the wounds of sin and division, and creates real communion.

February **19**

Christ's resurrection is the most overwhelming event in human history. This event gave everyone new hope. From now on, hope no longer means waiting for something to happen. It means being certain that something *has* happened because "the Lord is risen and reigns immortal."

It is time to overcome laziness and mediocrity, and to renew our whole life in the light of the Gospel.

February 21

February 22

*L*ook at yourselves from "within." Before being against a law or a moral norm, sin is against God (cf. Ps 50[51]:6), against your bothers and sisters, and against yourselves. Stand in front of Christ, only Son of the Father and Model for all brothers and sisters. He alone shows us what we must be in relation to the Father, to our neighbor, to society, in order to be at peace with ourselves.

$\mathcal{M}$ary's hope at the foot of the cross contains a light stronger than the darkness that reigns in many hearts; in the presence of the redeeming sacrifice, the hope of the Church and of humanity is born in Mary.

February 23

The wounds of humanity cannot leave us indifferent; we must heal, console, and care for the multitudes of suffering individuals and peoples.

The "power of the Gospel" appears in everyday life when in every context or circumstance there are courageous Christians who are not afraid to show their convictions.

February 25

*B*lessed are those who have not seen and have believed (cf. Jn 20:29). Jesus was thinking of those who would not see him risen, not eat and drink with him as the apostles had (cf. Acts 10:41), and yet would believe on the basis of eyewitness accounts. They are the ones in particular to be called "blessed" by Christ.

$\mathcal{T}$hrough the mystery of the Redemption, by the influence of the Holy Spirit, the Trinitarian mystery communicates to the Church the property of universalism. Thus the mystery of the Church derives from the mystery of the Trinity.

February 27

The Blessed Virgin is the model of Christian expectation and hope.

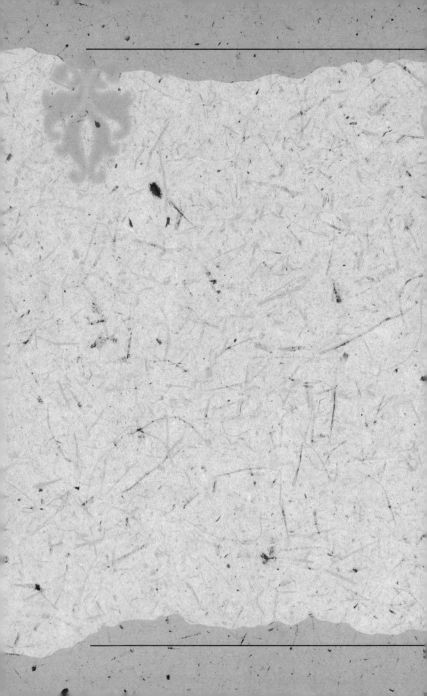

March

$\mathcal{T}$he rediscovery of the cardinal virtues and true ideals is extremely necessary today.

March 1

*P*eace is the gift of God! New hearts are first necessary if peace is to triumph in the world. Only the Good Shepherd can offer this newness of life, and he grants it to all those who listen to his words and follow him.

*T*he truth is that one cannot remain a prisoner of the past, for individuals and peoples need a sort of healing of memories so that past evils will not come back again. This does not mean forgetting past events; it means re-examining them with a new attitude and learning precisely from the experience of suffering that only love can build up, whereas hatred produces devastation and ruin. The deadly cycle of revenge must be replaced by the new-found liberty of forgiveness.

March 3

*D*o not be afraid;
Christ has overcome the world. He is with
all of you. May his peace always brighten
the horizons of your life.

The supernatural effectiveness of all your activity depends on the fervor of your "yes" to the word of God.

March 5

*L*ove, in a word, is the gift of self. This love, which is the great message of Christianity, is always replenished at the foot of the cross, before the overwhelming image of the Son of God incarnate who sacrifices himself for humanity's salvation.

$\mathcal{R}$emember always
that your field of apostolate is your own
personal life. Here is where the message of
the Gospel has first to be preached and
lived.

March 7

Everything begins
with the heart; here is where "conversion"
especially takes place, the conversion to
which we are called.

*I*t is Jesus who takes the initiative. When we have to deal with him, the question is always turned upside down: from questioners, we become the questioned; from "searchers," we discover that we are "sought." He, indeed, has always loved us first. This is the fundamental dimension of the encounter; we are not dealing with something, but with Someone, with the "Living One." Christians are not the disciples of a system of philosophy. They are men and women who, in faith, have experienced the encounter with Christ.

March **9**

*T*here is no doubt that following Christ is no easy undertaking. Indeed, Christian ethics point to an arduous path and invite us to enter by the narrow gate, the one that alone leads to true life.

*T*hroughout your life, follow the path of the Church, which I have often said is humanity's path! Keep firm in faith, strengthened in hope, united in love. These are the affectionate wishes which I entrust to Mary, the Mother of Jesus, who goes before us on the pilgrimage of faith.

March 11

$\mathcal{L}$ook to Jesus, the
living One, and repeat what the Apostles
asked: "Lord, teach us how to pray."
Prayer will be the salt that gives flavor to
your life, and leads you to Christ,
humanity's true light.

$\mathcal{T}$he maturing process of the person must be fostered; persons must be helped to develop their social, cultural, moral, and religious dimensions through the proper use of freedom.

March 13

Let it be love that builds bridges between us and encourages us to do everything possible. Let love for each other and love for the truth be the answer to present difficulties and questions.

$\mathcal{Y}$ou belong to Christ, and Christ belongs to you. At Baptism you were claimed for Christ with the Sign of the Cross; you received the Catholic faith as a treasure to be shared with others. In Confirmation, you were sealed with the gifts of the Holy Spirit and strengthened for your Christian mission and vocation. In the Eucharist, you receive the food that nourishes you for the spiritual challenges of each day.

March 15

*W*hen Jesus calls, it is
not to restrict a personality but to make it
unfold in its true essence so as to achieve
the ideal which motivates it.

To everyone, proclaim Christ who is the only fully satisfying answer to human expectations.

March 17

*I*t may not always be conscious and clear, but in the human heart there is a deep nostalgia for God. St. Ignatius of Antioch expressed this eloquently: "There is in me a living water that murmurs within me: *Come to the Father*" (*Ad. Range of motion*, 7).

$\mathcal{S}$ee what love the Father has given us, that we should be called children of God; and so we are (cf. 1 Jn 3:1). We are not orphans; love is possible. Because—as you know—we are not capable of loving if we are not loved.

March 19

God is preparing a
great springtime for Christianity, and we
can already see its first signs.

*H*oliness is not a sort of extraordinary ascetic journey which can only be undertaken by a few "geniuses," but…it is the "high standard" of ordinary Christian living (cf. *Novo Millennio Ineunte,* n. 31). Holiness is doing something beautiful for God every day, but also recognizing what God has done and continues to do in us and for us. Be holy, dear friends, because the lack of holiness is what makes the world sad!

March 21

We need to bring the Gospel of life to the heart of every man and woman and to make it penetrate every part of society.

$\mathcal{T}$he risen Christ returns among us with the fullness of joy and with overflowing richness of life. Hope becomes certainty, because if Christ has conquered death, we too can hope to triumph one day in the fullness of time, in the period of the final contemplation of God.

March 23

The certainty that God loves us makes us trust in God's fatherly providence even in life's most difficult moments. This complete trust in God, the providential Father, even in the midst of adversity, is admirably expressed by St. Teresa of Jesus: "Let nothing trouble you; let nothing frighten you. Everything passes. God never changes. Patience obtains all. Whoever has God wants for nothing. God alone is enough" (*Poems*, 30).

$\mathcal{M}$ary's "yes" at the Annunciation was necessary for the Word to take flesh in her womb. Your "yes" is necessary for Christ to take possession of your lives and make you apostles of his love.

$\mathcal{M}$arch 25

Even in the desert of daily life, the six workdays are made fruitful, illuminated, and sanctified by the meeting with God on the seventh day, through the liturgy and prayer of our ecclesial gathering on Sunday.

The sick or suffering bear Christ's cross. Each of them is a great prophet, a very great prophet who bears Christ's cross with his strength, in his light.

March 27

March 28

*I*n the Bread which
came down from heaven, the family will
be able to find the support that will keep
it united in the face of today's threats and
will preserve it as a bastion of life,
steadfast against the culture of death.

I invite you to reflect on what makes each one of you truly marvelous and unique. Only a human being like you can think and speak and share your thoughts in different languages with other human beings all over the world, and through that language express the beauty of art and poetry and music and literature and the theater, and so many other uniquely human accomplishments. And most important of all, only God's precious human beings are capable of loving.

March **29**

*J*ustice that endures is justice that is practiced humbly, compassionately sharing in the fate of others, sowing the spirit of pardon and mercy everywhere.

*B*y shining with faith, hope, and love, you will show Jesus Christ to others.

March 31

April

*I*nner peace comes
from knowing that one is loved by God
and from the desire to respond to that
love.

April 1

Why do we need Christ? Because Christ reveals the truth about man and woman…. He shows us our place before God, as creatures and sinners, as redeemed through his own death and Resurrection, as making our pilgrim way to the Father's house. He insists that there cannot be justice, brotherhood, peace, and solidarity without the Ten Commandments of the Covenant, revealed to Moses on Mount Sinai and confirmed by the Lord on the Mount of the Beatitudes (cf. Mt 5:3–12)….

*M*issionary endeavor reaches its goal when, in the power of the Spirit, it inspires in baptized persons an awareness of their "status" as children of God and awakens in them a more lively faith in Jesus, the only Savior, urging them to become witnesses and missionaries.

April 3

April 4

$\mathcal{M}$ay we in our daily lives break through the walls of the visible world in order to keep our eyes always and everywhere fixed on the Lord.

*L*ook to Mary! She welcomed the infinite mystery of the love of the Triune God in her person and in her life. Mary lived as a continuous Eucharist; she always remained intimately bound to Jesus and followed him faithfully.

April 5

"*Let* us forgive and let us ask for forgiveness." If Christ is to be our advocate with the Father, we cannot fail to utter these words. We cannot fail to undertake the difficult but necessary pilgrimage of forgiveness, which leads to a profound reconciliation.

A vocation is a gift from God, a gift for the person who receives it, and a gift for the whole Church as well (cf. *Pastores Dabo Vobis*, n. 41). It may be likened to a seed planted in the deepest part of a person's being. This seed needs to be watered and tended so that it may develop and grow. If given the proper attention and care, it will come to full maturity and bear much fruit in the Church and in the world.

April 7

April **8**

*J*esus is the faithful love
that does not abandon us and knows how
to turn the night into the dawn of hope. If
the cross is accepted, it generates
salvation and brings peace.

*M*ay young people discover in the heart of Christian homes the high noble ideals that will alleviate their deep-seated anxiety and protect them from the temptations of a culture devoid of solidarity or horizons, one that irreversibly leads to emptiness and discouragement.

April 9

April 10

*G*od conquers evil
with infinite mercy. It is in the face of this
merciful love that a desire for conversion
and a yearning for new life must be
reawakened in us.

*evive the age-old
roots of your faith; preserve and enrich
the precious heritage of your religious
traditions.*

April 11

*D*arkness can only be scattered by light. Hatred can only be conquered by love.

*I*n its reading of social problems, the Church stands in a vital spot which transcends the limits of human history in its purely temporal dimension. It never confuses the Kingdom of God with the construction of an earthly city.

April 13

"This is the work of the Lord, a marvel in our eyes" (Ps 118:23). Yes! We are the witnesses of the marvel, witnesses of the power of God. Divine power, which is life made manifest and communicated to give a new face to existence…; power that reveals goodness and condemns evil…; divine power which is the source of fresh vitality, capable of softening even hardened hearts and renewing courage in those who…wander aimlessly, pilgrims of the void; divine power, which is the condition of the true freedom for the human race, to whom it proclaims, today and always: Love has conquered hatred.

$\mathcal{L}$ove is beautiful
when it is true, when it can stand up to
the experiences and trials of life.

April 15

April 16

The rhythms of creation
are so many paths of extraordinary beauty
along which the sensitive, believing heart
easily catches the echo of the mysterious,
loftier beauty that is God the Creator, the
source and life of all reality.

*I*n order to learn to
love we need to communicate with God.

April 17

Prayer is a formidable weapon. In the human heart, it destroys the "wall" blocking God's love and fills in the chasms of hatred, distrust, and resentment that often cause divisions between individuals and peoples.

*T*he world you are inheriting is a world that desperately needs a new sense of human solidarity. It is a world that needs to be touched and healed by the beauty and richness of God's love. It needs witnesses to that love. The world needs salt. It needs you to be the salt of the earth and the light of the world.

April **19**

April 20

*May you be leaven
for the world, changing it from within,
especially by the example of your lives.*

"As the Father loves me, so I also love you. *Remain* in my love" (Jn 15:9). If you wish your unity to endure and not only to be linked to the enthusiasm of a particular moment, you must "remain" in Jesus' love as the branch remains joined to the vine.

April 21

*N*ever resign yourselves to lies, falsehood, or compromise! React strongly to those who attempt to ensnare your intelligence and lure your heart with messages and suggestions that make you slaves of consumerism, disordered sex, and violence, to the point of being driven into the void of loneliness and the meanders of the culture of death. Detached from truth, every freedom becomes a new and more burdensome slavery.

*I*n the course of their history, Christians have grown aware of the fact that celebration of the Eucharist could not be reduced to being kept within the walls of a church...but that it was necessary to take it out along the streets of the world.

April 23

April 24

Mary teaches us
how to listen to the word of God and put
it into practice in everyday life.

*I*n the mystery of the Church, all humanity draws near to God and shares in the peace brought by Christ. At the same time, all are summoned to work for a world of ever-greater reconciliation, justice, and peace.

April 25

*B*y conquering
death, Christ has made all things new (cf.
Rev 21:5). New life, new peace, and new
joy for all believers flow from Easter.

We must overcome our fear of the future. But we will not be able to overcome it completely unless we do so together.

April 27

*I*t is certainly impossible to comprehend the work of the Spirit in the Church and in the world by examining statistics or other means of human knowledge. It exists on another level, the level of grace perceived by faith. The Spirit's work is often hidden, mysterious, but always effective. The Holy Spirit has lost none of the propelling force manifested at the time of Jesus and the apostles.

Holiness is an ever-timely demand. Men and women today feel an urgent need for Gospel witnesses of life.

April 29

Christ gives us a sign: he calls us to hope in the resurrection and eternal life proclaimed by the whole of the Paschal Mystery. The Lord is my light and salvation. Our homeland is in heaven. Amen!

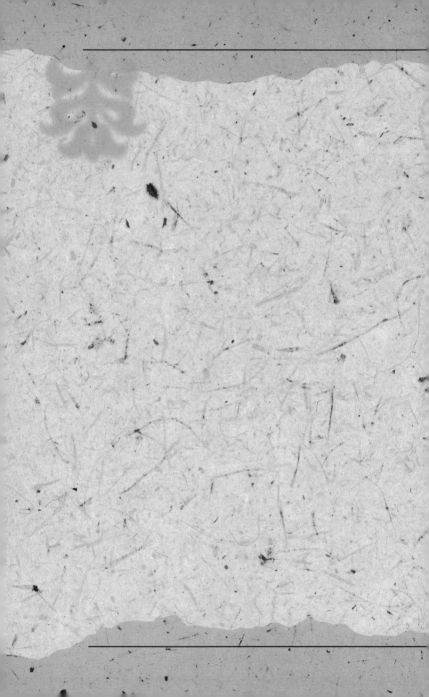

May

*A*t the Annunciation the Blessed Virgin welcomed the announcement of her divine motherhood. The "yes" she gave is the highest example of the "yes" every mother gives to the life of her baby.

May **1**

To be human is to go in search; all human searching is in the end a search for God. "Faith and reason are like two wings on which the human spirit rises to the contemplation of truth; and God has placed in the human heart a desire to know the truth—in a word, to know God—so that by knowing and loving God, men and women may also come to know the truth about themselves."

"God so loved the world that he gave his only Son, that whoever believes in him should not perish but have eternal life" (Jn 3:16). The world is loved by God!

May 3

$\mathcal{T}$he family is a place where a great effort is frequently required to witness to the Gospel in daily relations. Then at school, at work, in sports, in healthy entertainment, spread everywhere the peace and joy that Jesus gives his friends.

$\mathcal{F}$orgiving one's enemies, as the martyrs of all ages have done, is the decisive proof and authentic expression of the radical nature of Christian love. We must forgive because God forgives us and has renewed us in Christ. If we do not forgive completely, we cannot expect to be forgiven. On the other hand, if our hearts are open to mercy, if forgiveness is sealed with a fraternal embrace, and the bonds of communion are strengthened, we proclaim to the world the supernatural power of Christ's redemption.

May 5

What is the reason for our confidence, our trust, which should overcome fear? The Apostle Paul replies to us: "It is the gift of grace" that in Jesus Christ "overflows for the many."

*J*esus does not only look for people to acelaim him. He looks for people to follow him.

May 7

Very rightly we can
speak of the Church of the young,
remembering that the Holy Spirit renews
in everyone—even in the elderly,
provided they remain open and
receptive—the vibrancy of grace.

$\mathcal{C}$hrist is the One who constantly enters the Upper Room. He enters many upper rooms where people are fearful and discouraged like the Apostles after the trial of Good Friday. Christ enters and goes to meet the many "Thomases" of today, to convince them of his victory over death, of his love that gives peace, of the saving power of the redemption and of grace. We must be ready to welcome him, to "taste the kindness of the Lord" (cf. 1 Pt 2:3).

May 9

*H*uman life, the life
of the believer, is a continuous pilgrimage,
a pilgrimage of faith.

God seeks out all those who are suffering, who are marked by life's tribulations. God stands at their side, supports them and comforts them, offering to each one mercy, compassion, and genuine consolation.

May 11

*C*ommunion means living in Christ and letting Christ live in me, as the Apostle Paul expressed so powerfully (cf. Rom 6:10; Gal 2:20), to become, like him and in him, effective instruments in the loving plan of the Blessed Trinity, who through the Church wants to make one family of all people.

The cross reminds us of the price of our salvation. It speaks of what great value men and women have in God's eyes—every person!

May 13

Christ alone is the cornerstone on which it is possible solidly to build one's existence. Only Christ—known, contemplated, and loved—is the faithful friend who never lets us down, who becomes our traveling companion, and whose words warm our hearts (cf. Lk 24:13–35).

*T*oday there is a greatly felt need to slow down the sometimes hectic pace of our days. Contact with nature, with its beauty and its peace, gives us new strength and restores us. Yet, while the eye takes in the wonders of the cosmos, it is necessary to look into ourselves, into the depths of our hearts, into the center of our being, where we are face to face with our conscience. There, God speaks to us, and our dialogue with God gives meaning to our life.

May 15

May 16

Our God is
the God of joy!

*I*t is very important that the Christian community presents itself as a single body, diversified in functions and services, in groups and movements, but united in its motives, objectives, and Gospel style. It is the lesson of the Trinity.

May 17

*C*hrist is asking you
to be witnesses to peace and peacemakers.
Embrace this difficult but exalting
mission.

Christ has a place prepared for you. Indeed, he is himself the "place" for which your hearts yearn. Yes…yearn for Christ, love Christ! Love him with all the ardor of your hearts.…

May **19**

May 20

Christian hearts must always be open to the world, and the sufferings of their brothers and sisters. Even those who are far away cannot fail to involve them deeply.

*L*earn to remain with Christ, to be able to love like him. When you can during the week, take part in the Eucharist. Fidelity to the weekday Eucharist helps us to follow Christ in daily life, and gives us light and strength as we follow our vocation.

May 21

As the Father sent Christ, so Christ sends us to bring his message of love to the world. This is the light humanity needs. May we be the torches that bring it to the people of the third millennium.

As has happened throughout its history, the Church experiences persecution and martyrdom daily in many parts of the world, and the number of these witnesses is great. We should be aware of this; we are invited to show spiritual solidarity with those who by shedding their blood share in the destiny of Christ the Redeemer.

May 23

Remember: Christ is calling you; the Church needs you!

*A*uthentic and lasting conversion of heart cannot be brought about except in a spirit of prayer. Prayer is the bond which most effectively unites us: it is through prayer that believers meet one another at a level where inequalities, misunderstandings, bitterness, and hostility are overcome, namely before God, the Lord and Father of all.

May 25

The meeting with Jesus
is...the event which gives meaning to
human life and profoundly alters it, by
opening the spirit to horizons of authentic
freedom.

$\mathcal{H}$umanity is not
content with itself. There is now a
widespread conviction that the
domination of nature and the cosmos, the
most advanced science and technology do
not satisfy, because they are unable to
reveal the ultimate meaning of reality:
they are merely instruments, but not ends
for the life of the human person and the
journey of humanity.

May 27

The knowledge that the Spirit is at work in the hearts of believers and intervenes in the events of history is a reason for us to be optimistic and hopeful.

*M*issionary cooperation is primarily a faith event which gives first place to prayer, the offering of suffering, and witness of life, and is concretely expressed in many forms.

May 29

I repeat this invitation: open yourselves to God's greatest gift, to God's love which, through the cross of Christ, has revealed itself to the world as merciful love.... Continue to be "ready to bear witness to the cause of humanity." Today, with all my strength, I beseech the sons and daughters of the Church, and all people of good will: *never, ever separate "the cause of humanity" from the love of God.* Help modern men and women to experience God's merciful love! This love, in its splendor and warmth, will save humanity!

*M*ary's fullness of
grace reminds us of the immense
possibility for goodness, beauty, greatness
and joy which are within reach of human
beings when they let themselves be
guided by God's will and reject sin.

May 31

June

$\mathcal{L}$ove makes us seek what is good; love makes us better persons. It is love that prompts men and women to marry and form a family, to have children. It is love that prompts others to embrace the religious life or become priests. Love makes you reach out to others in need, whoever they are, wherever they are. Every genuine human love is a reflection of the love that is God, to the point where the First Letter of St. John says: "The man without love has known nothing of God; for God *is* love" (4:8).

June 1

*H*ow important it is
to discover authentic freedom! Not
everything that individuals or even whole
systems propose as an expression of
freedom is really such. A way must be
found to defend true freedom and to build
it up in truth day by day.

*I*n Jesus' love you will find the fulfillment of your deepest aspirations, and you will grow into full spiritual maturity.

June 3

"Enter through the narrow gate. The gate that leads to damnation is wide, the road is clear and many choose to travel it" (Mt 7:13). What is the "wide gate," what is the "clear road" of which Jesus speaks? It is the gate of moral autonomy, it is the road of intellectual pride. How many, even Christians, live in indifference, adopting a materialistic outlook and giving in to the allurements of sin!

*T*hrough prayer you
will learn to become light of the world,
because in prayer you become one with
the source of our true light, Jesus himself.

June 5

*I*ndeed, Jesus enters all aspects of everyone's life and vocation; he asks for consistent behavior in the experience of human love at school, at university, at work, in voluntary work, in sports, and in every other context of daily life. He gives meaning to joy and to sorrow, to health and to sickness, to poverty and to wealth, and to living and to dying.

$\mathcal{T}$oday, those who can live the Gospel consistently are swimming against the tide. This is the heroism of daily life, of living holiness at every instant and in every situation.

June 7

June 8

With deep conviction...I wish to appeal to everyone to seek peace along the paths of forgiveness. I am fully aware that forgiveness can seem contrary to human logic.... But forgiveness is inspired by the logic of love, that love which God has for every man and woman, for every people and nation.... If the Church dares to proclaim what, from a human standpoint, might appear to be sheer folly, it is precisely because of its unshakable confidence in the infinite love of God. As Scripture bears witness, the Father is rich in mercy and full of forgiveness for those who come back to him.

"*Jesus* loves you." These wonderful words are uttered within the heart of the believer who, like the disciple beloved of Jesus, rests his or her head on Jesus' breast and hears what is spoken in confidence: The ones who love me will be loved by my Father, and I will love them and manifest myself to them (cf. Jn 14:31).

June 9

All are searching,
though not all are looking in the right
place.

The Apostle Paul underscores reciprocal love between husband and wife, united not by a mere vow of fidelity, but by an indissoluble bond raised to a sacrament, a sign of Christ's union with the Church.

June 11

June 12

*I*t is more necessary
than ever to think and work in order to
incarnate lasting Gospel values in the new
social situation, so that it is not deprived
of its soul.

$\mathcal{L}$et us look at the Blessed Virgin's example. In the narrative of the wedding at Cana, John's Gospel offers us a vivid detail of her personality when it tells us how, in the busy atmosphere of a wedding feast, she alone realized that the wine was about to run out. And to avoid the spouses' joy becoming embarrassment and awkwardness, she did not hesitate to ask Jesus for his first miracle. This is the "genius" of woman!

June 13

June 14

Everywhere Christ
spreads the same message: Love one
another as I have loved you. And in the
Eucharist he offers himself as the spiritual
strength for putting this commandment
into practice and for building the
civilization of love.

What makes us holy is not work, but the action of grace within us. However, it does so over a whole lifetime and, therefore, within the specific limits of the daily toil by which we respond to grace.

June 15

Each one of you is being challenged to listen to the words of the Lord: "Whoever wishes to be my follower must deny his very self, take up his cross each day, and follow in my steps" (Lk 9:23): the cross of rejecting the ways of thinking that contradict the teachings of Jesus; the cross of rejecting desires and behavior that are not worthy of the followers of Christ. You are being invited to allow the transforming grace, which flows from the cross of Christ, to enter your lives—especially through the sacrament of Reconciliation.

$\mathcal{E}$vangelizers must patiently accept the times of evangelization, sometimes slow, sometimes even very slow, aware that God, to whom "the times and seasons" belong, tirelessly guides the course of history with sovereign wisdom.

June 17

June 18

$\mathcal{T}$he saints are those
who in every age know how courageously
to live their faith by bearing witness to
Christ without surrender or compromise.

$\mathcal{L}$ook for Jesus. Seek his presence in your lives and strive to know him ever more intimately. Do not be afraid to make yourselves known to him.

June 19

*V*ocation means
thinking of one's whole life as a response.

*I*t is good that people remember that they find themselves in a "flowerbed" of the immense universe created for them by God. It is important for people to realize that neither they nor the matters that they so frantically pursue are "everything." Only God is "everything," and in the end everyone will have to give an accounting of themselves to God.

June 21

Recognize life as a gift to be welcomed with gratitude, to be lived according to the law of God's love, and to be offered responsibly in service to one's brothers and sisters.

*I*ntimacy with God is the ultimate meaning and profound calling of every human life. When, in the Church, Jesus Christ calls men or women to follow him, he makes his voice heard and his fascination felt by the inner action of the Holy Spirit. To this Spirit, Christ entrusts the task of making his call understood and of awakening the desire to respond to it with a life entirely dedicated to Christ and his kingdom.

June 23

The believer must, like the Baptist, become a voice that proclaims the Lord's salvation, by fully adhering to the Gospel and witnessing to it visibly in the world.

The cross is written into men and women's lives. Wanting to exclude it from one's own life is like wanting to ignore the reality of the human condition. This is how it is! We are made for life, yet we cannot eliminate suffering and trials from our personal experience.... When there is no peace in the family, when it is almost impossible to find work, when plans for having a family have to be delayed, when you must contend with illness, loneliness and when there is a risk of falling prey to a dangerous emptiness of values...is it not the cross that challenges you?

June 25

June 26

*W*e must never be
ashamed of the Gospel and never be afraid
of proclaiming that we are Christians.
Instead we must continue to speak, to
extend the spaces for proclaiming
salvation, because Jesus has promised to
be with us forever and he is always in the
midst of his disciples.

*C*hrist is the truth
that can give direction to life and hope to
the future.

June 27

June 28

Suffering cannot be transformed and changed by a grace from outside, but from within…. However, this interior process does not always follow the same pattern…Christ does not answer in the abstract this human questioning about the meaning of suffering. Men and women hear Christ's saving answer as they gradually become sharers in the sufferings of Christ.

$\mathcal{T}$he human being is fully him or herself only when he or she meets God and can abandon self in the embrace of the Trinity! If you can follow this path, you will never be numbered among the masses, copies of the nameless faces of advertising.

June **29**

*L*et yourselves be
loved by Christ, in order to respond
bravely in turn, by loving him and loving
your brothers and sisters.

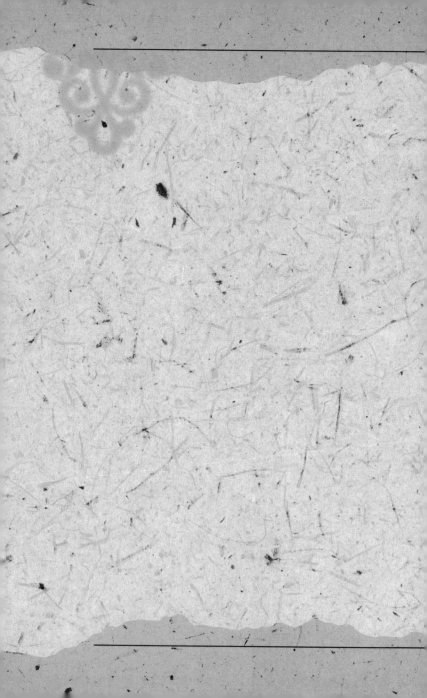

July

Authentic love is not a vague sentiment or a blind passion. It is an inner attitude that involves the whole human being. It is looking at others not to use them, but to serve them.

July **1**

$\mathcal{M}$ary is a teacher of prayer, life, and spirituality incarnated in human nature.

$\mathcal{D}$o not be afraid to open your hearts to Christ. Allow him to come into your lives, into your families, into society. In this way, all things will be made new. The Church repeats this appeal, calling everyone without exception—individuals, families, peoples—so that by faithfully following Jesus Christ all may find the full meaning of their lives.

July 3

*P*roclaim the Gospel of
love and justice to the world!

*P*rayer enables us to meet God at the most profound level of our being. It connects us directly to God, the living God: Father, Son, and Holy Spirit, in a constant exchange of love.

July 5

*I*n the intimacy of the tabernacle, the values that must reign in homes will receive new strength to make the family a meeting place with God, a center that radiates faith, a school of Christian life.

*D*ear brothers and sisters, it is not difficult to see that Sunday has an extraordinarily rich meaning. Its religious significance is not in opposition to the natural human values, which make it a time of rest, of enjoying nature and of more relaxed social relations. These are values that unfortunately risk being frustrated by a hedonistic and frenzied way of life. Living in the light of the Gospel, Christians impress their full meaning upon these values.

July 7

$\mathcal{E}$very quest of the human spirit for truth and goodness, and in the last analysis for God, is inspired by the Holy Spirit.

$\mathcal{L}$ooking to Christ, we make our own the words of a popular old Polish hymn: "Salvation came through the cross, this is a great mystery. All suffering has meaning: it leads to fullness of life."

July **9**

*L*et the Gospel be the measure and guide of life's decisions and plans! Then you will be missionaries in all that you do and say, and wherever you work and live you will be signs of God's love, credible witnesses to the loving presence of Jesus Christ. Never forget: "No one lights a lamp and then puts it under a bushel" (Mt 5:15)!

*D*o not let your hope die! Stake your lives on it! We are not the sum of our weaknesses and failures; we are the sum of the Father's love for us, and our real capacity to become the image of God's Son.

July 11

*A*bove all, vocation is a gift of God: it is not about choosing, but being chosen; it is the response to a love that precedes and accompanies.

*J*esus teaches us to place great confidence in God even in the most difficult moments. Nailed to the cross, Jesus abandons himself totally to the Father: "Father, into your hands I commit my spirit" (Lk 23:46). With this attitude he raises to a sublime level what Job had summed up in his famous words: "The Lord gave, and the Lord has taken away; blessed be the name of the Lord" (Jb 1:21). Even what is humanly a misfortune can be part of that great plan of infinite love in which the Father provides for our salvation.

July 13

July 14

People seek God
because they realize that God is seeking
them. The human heart yearns to meet
God and to rest in God.

$\mathcal{L}$et us learn to forgive! The spiral of hatred and violence, which bloodies the path of so many individuals and nations, can only be broken by the miracle of forgiveness.

July 15

*T*hrough Mary and with her help, you will be able to overcome the inevitable difficulties you will find along your way. With Mary you will be given the seed of Christ, the center and goal of every life, that you may plant it in the heart of every person you meet.

You have certainly heard of [Christ] since you were small, but let me ask you a question: Have you really met him? In faith have you had a living experience of him as a loyal and faithful friend, or does his image still seem too far removed from your real problems to excite any interest? Jesus is not only a great figure of the past, a teacher of life and morals. He is the risen Lord, the God who is close to every person, to whom we can speak and with whom we can experience the joy of friendship, hope in time of trouble, and the certainty of a better future.

July 17

$\mathcal{L}$ove for the truth
must be expressed in love for justice and
in the resulting commitment to
establishing the truth in relations within
human society.

*I*n contemplating the sublime figure of Mary most holy, in whom every state of life in the Church recognizes its own perfect model, we can also see the features of women's Gospel involvement in the world. May the Holy Spirit, who leads us into the fullness of truth (cf. Jn 16:13), lead each of you in the Blessed Virgin's footsteps to become ever more and ever better missionaries of God's infinite love.

July 19

*W*e love one another
truly and absolutely only when we love
forever in joy and in sorrow, in good times
and in bad.

$\mathcal{I}$n a world that offers easy pleasures and deceptive illusions, you must swim against the tide, taking your inspiration from the essential moral values, which alone can lead to a harmonious, prosperous, and peaceful life.

July 21

"*G*o and do not sin again" (Jn 8:11). [God's] pardon is given freely, but the person is invited to respond with a serious commitment to renewal of life.... So God's love is acted out in a continual offer of pardon.

*I*f your friendship with Christ, your knowledge of his mystery, your giving of yourselves to him are genuine and deep, you will be "children of the light," and you will become "the light of the world." For this reason I repeat to you the Gospel words: "Let your light so shine before others, that they may see your good works and give glory to your Father who is in heaven" (Mt 5:16).

July 23

Through the human person, spokesman for all creation, all living things praise the Lord. Our breath of life that also presupposes self-knowledge, awareness, and freedom (cf. Pr 20:27) becomes the song and the prayer of the whole of life that vibrates in the universe.

That is why all of us should address one another "with psalms and hymns and spiritual songs, singing and making melody to the Lord" with all our hearts (Eph 5:19).

God's work cannot be done by the lukewarm or half-hearted.

July 25

The path of the married couple and the family has two essential aspects: sanctification in a union of faithful love, and sanctification in fruitfulness, by fulfilling the task of raising their children as Christians.

*M*ay God be your only wealth: let yourself be molded by God, so that the holiness, truth, and love of the heavenly Father will become visible to our contemporaries, who are thirsting for real values.

July 27

*E*ach time we partake in the Holy Eucharist, we declare our belonging to Christ and our desire to be always his. We declare that we have thrown in our lot with Jesus since we have become one with him. We will do what he does, love what he loves, adopt his way of thinking, acting, living, his example and teaching as our very own.

$\mathcal{T}$hose who become too concerned and upset about things to be done are no longer able to communicate the value contained in that action, that is, God's love.

July 29

$\mathcal{T}$oday is not the time to hide the Gospel, but to "proclaim it on the housetops."

*M*ay his Gospel, his cross and resurrection, be ever alive in you. Be enamored of the Gospel. Every one of you will bear fruit—fruit "that remains"—to the extent that, through you, humanity will be brought closer to God, who is love, Omnipotence in Love. Is the modern person capable of understanding this truth? Are we too far distanced from it? Yes, Christ who sends you says: "All authority in heaven and on earth has been given to me." Be not afraid! You are sent in the power of Christ, in his power in heaven and on earth. Be not afraid!

July **31**

August

*E*very child that
comes into the world brings joy with it:
first of all joy for the parents and then for
the family and for the whole of humanity
(cf. Jn 16:21).

August 1

Do not be afraid…to open your time to Christ! Time given to Christ is not wasted; on the contrary, it is time gained for our humanity; it is time that fills our days with light and hope.

The Christian must learn to carry his or her cross with humility, trust, abandonment to God's will, finding in Christ's cross support and comfort amid life's troubles. May the Father grant that at every difficult moment we will be able to pray: *"Adoramus Te, Christe, et benedicimus tibi."* "We adore you, O Christ, and we bless you, because by your holy cross you have redeemed the world."

August 3

*B*ear witness to
Jesus. Place your hope firmly in him, and
let your words and deeds speak
courageously of this hope to others.

$\mathcal{T}$he Church needs your talents, your gifts, your enthusiasm. Be able to say "yes" to Christ who is calling you to be holy. "Holiness" is a demanding word, but should not frighten you. It does not imply doing extraordinary things but rather, living your own vocation really well, with the help of prayer, the sacraments, and a daily effort to be consistent. Yes, we need a generation of young people fascinated by the ideal of "holiness," if we wish to build a society worthy of the human person, a civilization of love.

August 5

*J*esus has a unique relationship with every person, which enables us to see in every human face the face of Christ.

*S*t. Paul says that Jesus crucified is our wisdom and our strength. It is a paradox, but this Crucified One is the source of all our strength, the strength of the suffering and of all those who do not want to err in life, who want to keep on the straight path, who want to build and not to destroy.

August 7

August 8

Let Christ involve you
in his mission. Do not make conditions
and reservations.

The human heart has depths from which schemes of unheard-of ferocity sometimes emerge, capable of destroying, in a moment, the normal daily life of a people. But faith comes to our aid when words seem to fail. Christ's word is the only one that can give a response to the questions that trouble our spirit. Even if the forces of darkness appear to prevail, those who believe in God know that evil and death do not have the final say. Christian hope is based on this truth....

August 9

*B*elievers know that,
in associating themselves with the
sufferings of Christ, they become
authentic workers for peace.

$\mathcal{L}$et Jesus present in the Blessed Sacrament speak to your hearts. It is he who is the true answer of life that you seek. He stays here with us: he is God-with-us. Seek Jesus without tiring, welcome him without reserve, love him without interruption: today, tomorrow, forever!

August 11

August 12

$\mathscr{Y}$our daily task is to give witness to the risen Christ among your peers, who need to give true meaning to their lives in the awareness that, because of the infinite love of Christ the Savior, a future rich in hope lies before them.

$\mathcal{E}$ven in darkness and in emptiness we can find the fullness of light and life, since from the cross alone come the light, the order, and the fullness of God for which all men and women long. There alone does the human heart find rest.

August 13

"To give my life": this
is the only ideal worthy to be lived to the
end, whatever the cost. This is also the
way of joy, as Jesus said: "It is more
blessed to give than to receive" (Acts
20:35).

$\mathcal{W}$alk to Mary. Walk with Mary. Let her take you by the hand, as children are led by a Mother. Watch her like the "star" of your journey. Make her "fiat" echo in your hearts.

August 15

There are two concepts that surpass human understanding: the first is that God became a human person; the second is that this God-man wished to suffer, be crucified, buried, and on the third day to rise again. To take this step, to arrive at faith, human knowledge alone is not enough, nor is philosophy, nor all the sciences. Prayer is required. Faith is required, and faith always implies prayer.

$\mathcal{L}$et us not be
overwhelmed by the distress of the
present time. Let us instead open our
hearts and minds to the great challenges
lying before us.

August 17

What is the way to live and communicate Christ's truth and joy without fear? The way, beloved, is the same way that Jesus took: the way of service, sharing, and the gift of one's own life.

$\mathcal{O}$ld age is also a gift for which we are called to give thanks: a gift for the person on in years, for society, and for the Church. Life is always a great gift.

*R*edeemed humanity is involved in a complex dynamic. God is not satisfied with a conditional response. God wants total commitment. . . . A few acts of generosity are not enough to satisfy the demands arising for those who have been ontologically reborn through Christ. Paul the Apostle's discourse on this subject is very clear: by Baptism, we have been re-born so that, as Christ was raised from the dead by the glory of the Father, we too might walk in newness of life (cf. Rom 6:4).

In the life-giving wood
of the cross, we rediscover our roots.

August 21

Today too, Mary's light can spread throughout the world of woman, to embrace woman's old and new problems, helping everyone to understand her dignity and to recognize her rights.

*F*asting means being
able to give up things, to go without them
for a higher spiritual motive. It means
living as a spiritual person rather than as a
materialistic one.

August 23

Let us show the whole world Christ crucified as our wisdom and our strength. Look to him; do not ignore him!

$\mathscr{T}$ruth is not always easy: its affirmation is sometimes quite demanding. Nevertheless, it must always be respected in human communication and human relations.

August 25

*T*he poor, the sick, the elderly who have been neglected, prisoners, those with physical or psychological disabilities, those enslaved by drug addiction, those marginalized because of unemployment, the young without horizons of hope, are numerous forms of the challenging presence of Christ, whom we worship in the Eucharist.

$\mathcal{P}$ersevere in prayer, which is praise, entreaty, and personal dialogue with the heavenly Father present in our hearts. Time spent in dialogue with the Lord is never time lost.

August 27

Evangelization based on the Eucharist entails a commitment to put the Church's social teaching into practice by promoting justice, particularly for our neediest brothers and sisters.

The cross, in which the glorious face of the risen Christ already shines, introduces us to the fullness of Christian life and perfect love, because it reveals Christ's longing to share with us God's very life, love, holiness. In the light of this mystery, the Church remembers the words of the Lord: *"Be perfect, as your heavenly Father is perfect"* (cf. Mt 5:48). The Church understands ever more clearly that its mission would be senseless if it did not lead to…perfect love and holiness. Contemplating the cross we learn to live with humility and forgiveness, peace and communion.

August 29

oday…in our restless and often confused world, *silence* helps us to make space for the word which saves, *listening* teaches us attention and tenderness, while free and generous *service* enlivens fraternal and community life.

$\mathcal{Y}$ou share the joys and hopes of the people who live close to you and with you: you are part of them and with them you must hope and work for a better future for all. Be cautious, but have the courage to make things new.

August 31

September

$\mathcal{C}$hrist is closer to us
than we can imagine. He identifies himself
with us, making us share his divine life
and mission.

September 1

September 2

Peace is possible! It is possible because men and women have a conscience and a heart. It is possible because God loves each one of us just as each one is, so as to transform and make him or her grow.

*S*ave the family, and
you will have saved society.

September 3

September 4

What should be our attitude to God's providential and far-sighted action? We certainly should not wait passively for what God sends us, but cooperate in bringing to completion the work already begun in us. We must be eager to seek first the things of heaven.

$\mathcal{S}$uffering is a mystery, often inscrutable to reason. It is part of the mystery of the human person, which is only explained in Jesus Christ, the One who reveals to the human person his or her own identity. Only through Jesus will we find the meaning of all that is human.

September 5

*H*oliness, a gift to be constantly requested, constitutes the most precious and effective response to the modern world's hunger for hope and life.

Come out and go to meet God, who is the Creator, your Creator, to whom everything owes its existence. This is the prime, fundamental call to understanding enlightened by faith. Indeed, it is the prime invitation to understanding sincerely, to seeking the truth along the paths of science and philosophical reflection.

September 7

That which makes human words capable of helping souls is the grace of God.

The Father gave Christ to the world so that man and woman would not be lost on the tangled paths of their pilgrimage, but would have eternal life (cf. Jn 3:16).

September 9

September 10

*W*hen we feel loved, we ourselves are more disposed to love. When we experience God's love, we are more ready to follow the One who loved his disciples…to the point of the total gift of himself. It is this love that humanity needs, today perhaps more than ever, because *love alone is credible.* It is the unshakable faith in this love that in every age…opens broad horizons of forgiveness and harmony…. Everything is possible to those who let themselves be transformed by the grace of Christ's Spirit, poured into our hearts with Baptism (cf. Rom 5:5).

*G*od is a rock, a fortress, in which we find refuge. God is a shield and a stronghold, the power of salvation. God never disappoints the expectations of those who call out in moments of trial.

September 11

September 12

The Gospel proclamation must always be renewed. It must become ever more complete and profound, even in regions and cultures evangelized long ago. It must begin again every day, until the coming of the "last day" (cf. Jn 12:48).

Love is acquired in spiritual effort.

September 13

September 14

However twisted and confused the course of history may appear, we know that, by walking in the footsteps of the crucified Nazarene, we shall attain the goal. Amid the conflicts of a world often dominated by selfishness and hatred, we, as believers, are called to proclaim the victory of Love.

$\mathcal{M}$ary is the voice of courage and pride: she will urge you on. She is the hand of a loving mother: she will sustain you.

September 15

September 16

With the interior
gaze of the soul, men and women can
discover that the world is not silent but
speaks of the Creator, when their interior
spiritual vision, their religious intuition,
is not taken up with superficiality. As the
ancient sage says: "From the greatness and
beauty of created things their original
author is seen by analogy" (Wis 13:5).

$\mathcal{W}$ith God nothing is impossible! What is especially possible is conversion, which can change hatred into love and war into peace.

September 17

September 18

*H*old fast to this certainty: [God is] the only one that can give meaning, strength, and joy to life. "God's love will never leave you, God's covenant of peace will never be removed from you" (cf. Is 54:10). "God has stamped your name on the palms of his hands" (cf. Is 49:16).

$\mathcal{E}$nter again into
yourself. Yes, we must enter again into
ourselves if we want to find ourselves. Not
only our spiritual life is at stake but
indeed our personal, family, and social
equilibrium itself.

September 19

The "little ones": how different is human logic from the divine! The "little ones," according to the Gospel, are those who know they are God's creatures and shun all presumption: they expect everything from God and so are never disappointed. This is the basic attitude of the believer: faith and humility are inseparable. The greater one's faith, the "littler" one feels, in the image of Jesus Christ, who, "though he was in the form of God, emptied himself" (cf. Phil 2:6–7) and came among us as our servant.

$\mathcal{T}$rue life is to
progressively attain self-control. Root
your hope and your faith in Christ.

September *21*

*L*et us entrust to the Blessed Virgin those who are going through periods of confusion and doubt, which make them feel there are no certitudes or hope. At the same time, let us learn humility and boldness from Mary so that we can always advance toward the truth, seeking it and bearing witness to it with all our strength. May she help us understand that the search for truth, in the last analysis, is a search for God.

When Jesus died on the cross in his terrible passion, humiliated and abandoned, he showed to the whole world the full meaning and depth of such trials.

September 23

September 24

*F*aith must be
constantly strengthened through frequent
meditation on God's word.

$\mathcal{S}$unday is the day of faith par excellence; a day on which believers, contemplating the face of the risen Christ, are called to repeat with Thomas: My Lord and my God! (Jn 20:28), and to relive in the Eucharist the Apostles' experience when the Lord entered the Upper Room and gave them the gift of the Spirit.

September 25

September 26

*I*n the Eucharist, the
community is gathered together by the
Lord its head and receives nourishment to
complete its own journey with consistency.

*P*oured out into the human heart, the Spirit makes the whole Blessed Trinity present within the human person. This indwelling, which springs from love and enriches love, demands to be expressed in truth.

September 27

September 28

*P*arents and families of
the whole world, let me say to you: God
calls you to holiness! God has chosen you
"before the creation of the world,"
St. Paul tells us, to "be holy and blameless
before him...through Jesus Christ"
(Eph 1:4). God loves you passionately and
desires your happiness, but God wants
you to be always able to combine fidelity
with happiness, because one cannot exist
without the other.

*I*t is necessary to be with young people, to give them high and noble ideals, to make them feel that the Lord can satisfy the yearning of their hearts.

September 29

Calling upon the
"Father" is the secret, the breath, the life
of Jesus.

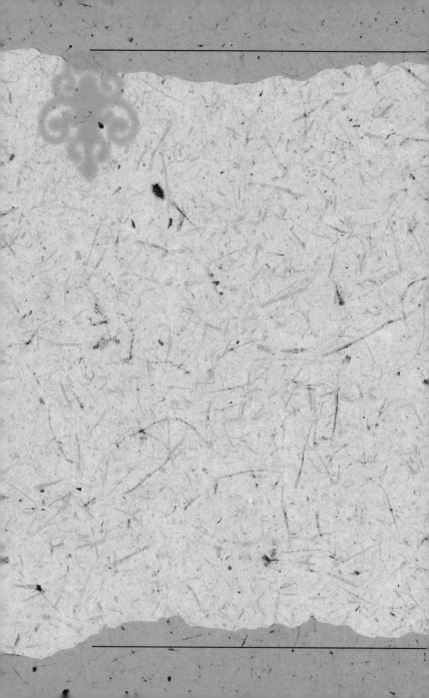

October

"I offer you praise, O Father, Lord of heaven and earth, because what you have hidden from the learned and the clever you have revealed to the merest children" (Lk 10:21). This marvelous blessing, which springs from Christ's heart, reminds us that genuine intellectual maturity always goes hand in hand with simplicity. The latter does not consist in a superficiality of life and thought nor in denial of the problematic nature of reality, but rather in knowing how to go to the heart of every question and to discover its essential meaning and relationship to the whole. Simplicity is wisdom.

October 1

October 2

*W*hat could seem to human eyes a slow and uneven path, is actually God's method.

*K*eep the Christian faith, announce it in word and deed, help others to believe that God is the merciful Father of all humanity, that Jesus Christ is the Savior in whom we are reborn to new life, that the Holy Spirit is the guiding force of our lives.

October 3

*M*any false teachers point out dangerous ways that lead to fleeting joys and satisfactions. Today expressions of culture are often mired in superficiality. Refuse to sell your dreams too cheaply! Dream, but in freedom! Plan, but in truth!

*T*he message of merciful love needs to resound forcefully anew. The world needs this love. The hour has come to bring Christ's message to everyone: to rulers and the oppressed, to those whose humanity and dignity seem lost in the *mysterium iniquitatis* [mystery of sin]. The hour has come when the message of Divine Mercy is able to fill hearts with hope and to become the spark of a new civilization: the civilization of love.

October 5

October **6**

$\mathcal{I}$ ask you not to be discouraged...; your call to holiness is a precious adornment of the Church. Believe in your vocation. Be faithful to it. "God has called you and will not fail you."

*C*ontemplating with Mary the joyful, sorrowful, and glorious mysteries of Christ the Lord, we can find the light and strength we need to fulfill the loving plan which God has for each of us.

October 7

*E*ven if human
works fade, hope in God never fails!

"Come to me, all you who are weary and find life burdensome, and I will refresh you" (Mt 11:28). We are not afraid to come before Christ with the burden of our infidelities: Christ is the Redeemer!

October **9**

*B*e humble instruments, simple and detached from yourselves and your activities. Be firmly bound to Christ and his words alone. Thus, you will be able to scatter seeds of unity, reconciliation and dialogue in the various contexts where you live and work.

Those who "remain" in God's love "bear much fruit" (cf. Jn 15:5). The first "fruit" the disciples bear is precisely to be one, loving one another as Jesus loved them (cf. Jn 15:12).

October 11

October 12

*L*et the whole Church
pray for vocations with trusting hope,
aware that vocations are a gift to be
begged for with prayer and to be merited
with holiness of life.

*P*ay attention to what unites rather than to what divides and grow in the quest for the truth: you will find greater possibilities for friendship; you will find new opportunities for co-operation and dialogue; you will be more attentive to the needs of the poor; your deep desire to share in spiritual and material goods will be greatly increased. Fraternal charity alone will ensure that those who are wealthy do not shut themselves off in selfishness and that those who are poor do not feel humiliated by their poverty.

October 13

October 14

*L*ove is the only
power that opens hearts to the word of
Jesus and to the grace of redemption. It is
the only power able to lead us to share as
brothers and sisters all that we are and all
that we have through Christ's will.

*P*eace is the great gift of the Lord. But conversion of heart is necessary to receive it.

October 15

*Y*our "yes"…has to be ever reaffirmed to the Lord. This requires a daily listening and probing and responding to his crucified—and crucifying—love. …Only Christ is able through the Spirit to overcome the weakness experienced time and again. Even Mary's "yes," which she spoke in a unique decision, had to be repeated over and over again, until she was standing beneath the cross where she offered her Son and became our Mother. God…also wants your "yes." Say it every day anew—then it will be true for you too—"Blessed is she who has believed."

$\mathcal{W}$e are the people
of life and *for* life, and this is how we
present ourselves to everyone.

October **17**

$\mathcal{L}$oving Christ is your answer to his love for you; it is to respond to what he says to you, especially in the Scriptures and in the teaching of the Church.

$\mathcal{L}$earn to place the Eucharist at the center of your life. By meditating on the Gospel, you will deepen your understanding of its meaning. This will help you to rediscover the value and beauty of the Sunday Eucharistic assembly, the joy of belonging to a people who carry the crucified and risen Christ in their hearts.

October **19**

October 20

*H*ow can we fail to
see the work of divine Providence, which
guides humanity and history toward more
dignified conditions of life for all people?

*T*he human person, aided and strengthened by supernatural grace, is actually capable of surpassing self. Hence, certain demands of the Gospel, which from a purely earthly and temporal viewpoint could seem too hard, are not only possible but can even result in bringing essential benefits to a person's growth in Christ.

October 21

This is the Church's missionary path: to go to meet women and men of every race, tongue, and nation with friendship and love, sharing their conditions in an evangelical spirit, to break the bread of truth and charity for them.

*O*nly love can truly
make two young people understand that
they are called to walk through life
together.

*O*ctober *23*

*T*he divine Teacher, before dawn or after sunset, and in other decisive moments of his mission, loved to retire alone to a solitary and silent spot so as to be alone with his heavenly Father and to talk to him. In these moments, he certainly did not fail to contemplate creation, to find in it a reflection of divine beauty.

*A*lways look trustingly toward Jesus, the "Suffering Servant," asking him for the strength to transform the trial afflicting you into a gift. Listen with faith to Jesus' voice repeating to each of you: "Come to me, all who are weary and oppressed, and I will give you rest" (Mt 11:28).

October 25

*O*ctober *26*

*M*ake yourselves
saints and do so quickly!

*J*esus rejoices over the divine fatherhood; he rejoices because his task is to reveal this fatherhood, and he is pleased lastly because of a particular effect of this fatherhood on the childlike.

October 27

October 28

*B*ear witness that the
serious problems of today can be solved if
we succeed in making Jesus Christ present
among people.

$\mathcal{M}$ary cooperated in the development of Jesus' mission by giving birth to him, raising him, being close to him in his hidden life; and then, during the years of his public ministry, by discretely supporting his activities, beginning with Cana when she obtained the first demonstration of the Savior's miraculous power.

October **29**

*P*recisely because evil is still lodged in many hearts and sin is the ultimate cause of personal and social disorder, of all selfishness and oppression, of violence and revenge, it is necessary for Christians to engage in fostering the task of teaching peace by practicing forgiveness. Thus, they will make themselves worthy of Jesus' beatitude: "Blessed are the peacemakers, for they shall be called sons of God" (Mt 5:9).

The Gospel vocation is a calling to live in God.

October 31

November

$\mathcal{L}$et us look to the saints who are valiant witnesses of fidelity to Christ; let us be inspired by their example in climbing the mountain of holiness. Be saints! This—as you well know—is every believer's calling.

November 1

November 2

The truth about men and women, which the modern world finds so hard to understand, is that we are made in the image and likeness of God's own self (cf. Gn 1:27). ...But what is even more difficult for contemporary culture to understand is that this dignity, already forged in the creative act of God, is raised immeasurably higher in the mystery of the incarnation of the Son of God. This is the message that you have to proclaim to the modern world: especially to the least fortunate, ...to those who suffer...:. To each one you must say: Look to Jesus Christ in order to see who you really are in the eyes of God!

Every true love supposes sacrifice and pain and lifelong commitment.

November 3

*D*o not fear to take Mary as your mother on the journey of life! May Mary be a model for you of how to follow Jesus. Do not be afraid of confiding in her, of entrusting to her maternal hands every problem, every anxiety, every expectation, and every project.

*M*y wish is that you will continue to deepen your awareness that Christ is our Way, our Truth, and our Life (cf. Jn 14:6).

November 5

*D*o not be afraid to welcome Christ in your homes, your offices, your stores, your factories, your farms and craft centers, your schools and places of recreation and sport. Do not be afraid to make room for the Father, who helped humanity to the extent that he wished his Son to share, with Mary and Joseph, a normal family life and to share with them their daily toil necessary for earning their bread.

God's plans do not coincide with those of human beings; they are infinitely better, but often incomprehensible to the human mind.

November 7

*B*e witnesses of
hope: a hope that looks to the future
without subjecting itself to numerous
daily problems, but founded on the
certitude of God's presence.

$\mathcal{B}$y knowing the Gospel, you will encounter Christ. Do not be afraid of what he may ask of you. Instead, thank God because Christ is demanding! He is demanding! When I was young…Christ was demanding and he convinced me. Were he not demanding, there would be nothing to listen to, to follow. But if Christ is demanding, it is because he offers values and it is the values he preaches that are demanding.

November 9

I invite all the faithful, priests and religious to pray tirelessly that the Lord of the harvest will send laborers into his vineyard (cf. Mt 9:37–38).

*A*t the end of our life we will be judged on love, on the acts of charity we have done to the least of our brothers and sisters (cf. Mt 25:31–45), but also on the courage and fidelity with which we have witnessed to Christ.

November 11

November 12

We would be
succumbing to a false strategy if we tried
to make complaining about today's world
and warning against its temptations the
center of our life and activity.

The "spirit of the world" offers many false illusions and parodies of happiness. There is perhaps no darkness deeper than the darkness that enters young people's souls when false prophets extinguish in them the light of faith and hope and love. The greatest deception, and the deepest source of unhappiness, is the illusion of finding life by excluding God, of finding freedom by excluding moral truths and personal responsibility. The Lord calls you to choose between these two voices competing for your souls.

November 13

November 14

Mary is the source of comfort and hope for all believers.

This work of giving their children moral and spiritual formation sanctifies parents, who are thus blessed with a deeper, renewed faith.

November 15

November 16

The rediscovery of Sunday is one of the urgent priorities in the life of the Christian community today. For many people, in fact, this day risks being considered and lived merely as the "weekend." But Sunday is quite different; it is the day of the week when the Church celebrates Christ's resurrection. It is the weekly Easter!

Called to union with Christ and to suffer like Christ, the Christian announces the constructive power of the cross with the acceptance and the offering of suffering.

November 17

Since we have received this life freely, we must in turn offer it freely to our brothers and sisters. This is what Jesus asked of the disciples when he sent them out as his witnesses in the world: "You received without paying, give without pay." And the first gift to be given is the gift of a holy life, bearing witness to the freely given love of God.

$\mathcal{T}$he Church entrusts to young people the task of proclaiming to the world the joy that springs from having met Christ.

November **19**

$\mathcal{L}$isten with gratitude and wonder to the amazing revelation of Jesus: "The Father loves you!" (cf. Jn 16:27). "These are the words I entrust to you. Receive the love that God first gives you" (cf. 1 Jn 4:19).

$\mathcal{W}$ith all my heart, I once again entrust my life and ministry to the Virgin Mary, Mother of the Redeemer and Mother of the Church. To her I repeat with filial abandonment: *Totus tuus!* Amen.

November 21

November 22

*T*he Christian life is a continuous struggle for the coming of God's kingdom, which entered human history and was definitively accomplished by Christ. However, that kingdom is not of this world; it belongs to the Father and only the Father can make it present among men and women. To them is given the task of being fertile ground in which the kingdom can develop and grow. Sometimes it is necessary to make great sacrifices and suffer persecution in order that this may happen.

$\mathscr{W}$ork offers us the place, the environment, the means or the tools and language of our response to the caring love of God.

November 23

We need to believe in Jesus, trust him, and love him. All this cannot happen unless we know him enough. Each of us has to find his/her own answer to the question Jesus put to his disciples, and now puts to each one of us: But you, who do *you* say I am? (Mt 16:15)

$\mathscr{P}$eace depends on solidarity of soul. This implies the courage to forgive. It is essential to know how to ask forgiveness and how to forgive.

November 25

November 26

When we are shaken by the sight of evil spreading in the universe...we should not forget that such unleashing of the forces of sin is overcome by the saving power of Christ. Whenever the words of consecration are uttered in the Mass and the body and blood of Christ become present in the act of the sacrifice, the triumph of love over hatred, of holiness over sin, is also present. Every Eucharistic celebration is stronger than all the evil in the universe; it means real, concrete accomplishment of the redemption....

$\mathcal{R}$ecognize the extraordinary gift of Christ, who comes to dwell in your whole being and make your heart and body a pleasing temple to him.

November 27

November 28

*D*ear people who are sick, be able to find in love the salvific meaning of your sorrow and the valid answers to all of your questions. Yours is a mission of most lofty value for both the Church and society. You who are weighed down by suffering are in the front line of those beloved by God. Just as Christ looked on all those whom he met on the roads of Palestine, he looks on you with eyes full of tenderness. His love will never fail.

Teach the law of Christian love! Supernatural charity breaks the recurring chains of hatred and revenge.

November 29

November 30

Faith accompanied by good works is contagious and spreads light, for it makes God's love visible and communicates it. Strive to make this lifestyle your own, listening to the Apostle Peter's words proclaimed in the Scriptures (cf. 1 Pt 3:15). He urges believers always to answer with great readiness "to anyone who asks you to account for the hope that is in you," and adds, "it is better to suffer for doing good, if that should be God's will, than for doing evil" (1 Pt 3:17).

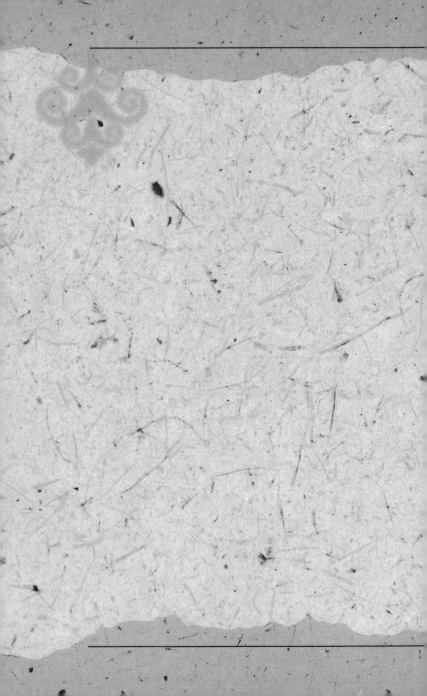

December

$\mathcal{D}$o not be content with anything less than the highest ideals! Do not let yourselves be dispirited by those who are disillusioned with life and have grown deaf to the deepest and most authentic desires of their heart. You are right to be disappointed with hollow entertainment and passing fads, and with aiming at too little in life. If you have an ardent desire for the Lord, you will steer clear of the mediocrity and conformism so widespread in our society.

December 1

God made us for joy.
God is joy, and the joy of living reflects the
original joy that God felt in creating us.

$\mathcal{G}$od's presence in us is the basis of our existence. The road of interiority and contemplation is not for the chosen few, but for every authentic believer.

December 3

December 4

Serve Christ in your
family and friends, and in all those you
meet on life's path.

The Father has poured out the Spirit in abundance on his adoptive children, manifesting in the various forms of consecrated life a fatherly love, which he wishes to extend to the whole of humanity. God continues to point out the expectations of eternal life which open the heart to hope, even in the midst of difficulties, pain and death, especially by means of those who leave everything to follow Christ, dedicating themselves totally to the establishment of the kingdom.

December 5

What is holiness if
not the joyous experience of God's love
and meeting God in prayer?

$\mathcal{W}$hen we are in the "valley of tears," let us walk keeping our eyes fixed on the bright goal of peace and communion. Let us repeat in our hearts the final beatitude, which is like an antiphon that seals the Psalm: "O Lord of hosts, blessed is the one who trusts in you!" (83:13).

December 7

We ask the Blessed Virgin to help us to be aware of the beauty of God's plan. In the special mission entrusted to her, Mary brought all her feminine richness first to the family of Nazareth and later to the first community of believers. May the men and women of our time learn from her the joy of being fully themselves, establishing mutual relations of respectful and genuine love.

*F*idelity to Christ requires a firmness that can reach the point of bloodshed.

December **9**

To use suffering to advantage and to offer it for the salvation of the world are themselves an action and mission of peace. From the courageous witness of the weak, the sick, and the suffering the loftiest contribution to peace can flow forth.

$\mathcal{L}$et us ask ourselves whether we do not at times relativize the truths of faith even as we absolutize the ideologies of this world. It is with the Gospel that we must judge the world, never accommodating the message of Christ to the opinions of the day.

December 11

December 12

*M*ary is the Mother of God, Mother of the Church and, in this Church, the mother of all people and all nations. Mary is with us. Everyone looks to her: her divine motherhood has become the great patrimony of humanity.

$\mathcal{L}$et no one mislead you or prevent you from seeing what really matters. Turn to Jesus, listen to him, and discover the true meaning and direction of your lives.

December 13

December 14

The new Life that has burst forth in the resurrection is the world's only hope. In the name of Christ, in the name of needy humanity: I encourage you to have that new Life in you! Be witnesses of that new Life to the world around you.

*I*n your daily life, you are called to make choices that "occasionally demand uncommon sacrifices." This is the price of true happiness.

December 15

December 16

This is the condition of the true Christian, who can nurture a trustful optimism, because he or she is certain of not walking alone. In sending us Jesus, the eternal Son-made-man, God has drawn near to each of us. In Christ, God has become our traveling companion. If time marches on inexorably, often shattering even our dreams, Christ, the Lord of time, gives us the possibility of an ever-new life.

$\mathcal{I}$n this crucible of the "Love of loves," will be forged the apostolic spirit of lay Christians, witnesses to Christ amid temporal realities.

December 17

*T*he persuasive power of the message also depends on the credibility of its messengers. Indeed, the new evangelization starts with us, with our lifestyle. The Church today does not need part-time members, but full-blooded Christians.

*A*dmiration of creation, admiration of God's work, is so necessary. Through admiring creation, we admire God; through admiring the visible, we admire the invisible.

December 19

December 20

*I*n our time; which is secularized yet also fascinated by the search for the sacred, there is a particular need to be saints who, by living intensely the primacy of God in their lives, make visible God's loving and provident presence.

*C*hrist is our peace!
How fragile is a peace not rooted in the
eternal, not based on the sure foundation
of God's law and love.

December 21

The word of God, the truth of faith, is not professed merely in words, but also through deeds, indeed, above all through deeds.

$\mathcal{L}$et yourselves be "formed" in the school of Jesus. In the Church and in the various environments of your daily existence, become credible witness to the Father's love! Make it visible in your choices and attitudes, in your way of accepting people and placing yourselves at their service, in faithfully respecting God's will and commandments.

December **23**

December 24

*L*ove Jesus. Give
yourselves to him in prayer; receive him
in the sacraments; worship him in the
assembly of the faithful.

*C*hrist is the answer
to our deepest expectations.

December **25**

December 26

*C*hrist is asking you
to get to know him and to meet him,
because after experiencing comforting
intimacy with him, you will be able to
proclaim the marvels of God's love to all.

The Christian faithful are called to build a "new world," transforming with charity and Gospel values the social structures that deny or contradict the truth about God and humanity.

December 27

There is a way of living the cross with bitterness and sadness, but it breaks our spirit. There is also the way of carrying the cross as Christ did, and then we perceive clearly that it leads to glory.

Closeness to Christ in silence and contemplation does not distance us from our contemporaries but, on the contrary, makes us attentive and open to human joy and distress and broadens our heart on a global scale.

December **29**

May Mary and Joseph of Nazareth, artisans of the family and life, be models and guides for young people, married couples, and the elderly in all families.

*T*hroughout the whole world the Church courageously proclaims: Open the doors to Christ! He has come so that all will have life in abundance.

December 31

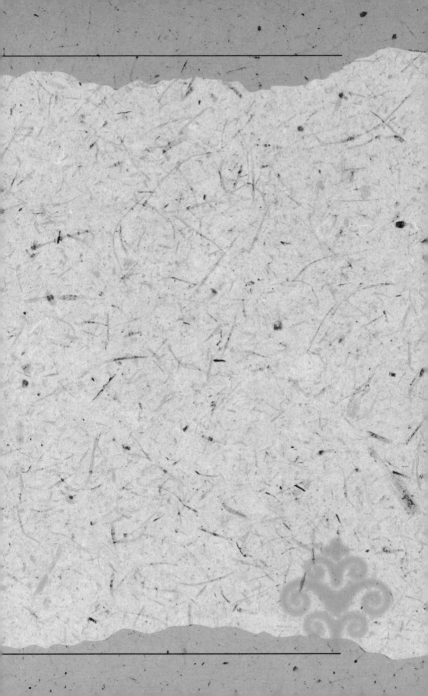

BOOKS & MEDIA

The Daughters of St. Paul operate book and media centers at the following addresses. Visit, call or write the one nearest you today, or find us on the World Wide Web, www.pauline.org

CALIFORNIA

3908 Sepulveda Blvd, Culver City,
CA 90230   310-397-8676

5945 Balboa Avenue, San Diego,
CA 92111   858-565-9181

46 Geary Street, San Francisco,
CA 94108   415-781-5180

FLORIDA

145 S.W. 107th Avenue, Miami,
FL 33174   305-559-6715

HAWAII

1143 Bishop Street, Honolulu,
HI 96813   808-521-2731

Neighbor Islands call:
1-866-521-2731

ILLINOIS

172 North Michigan Avenue,
Chicago, IL 60601   312-346-4228

LOUISIANA

4403 Veterans Memorial Blvd,
Metairie, LA 70006   504-887-7631

MASSACHUSETTS

885 Providence Hwy, Dedham,
MA 02026   781-326-5385

MISSOURI

9804 Watson Road, St. Louis,
MO 63126   314-965-3512

NEW JERSEY

561 U.S. Route 1, Wick Plaza,
Edison, NJ 08817   732-572-1200

NEW YORK

150 East 52nd Street, New York,
NY 10022   212-754-1110

78 Fort Place, Staten Island,
NY 10301   718-447-5071

PENNSYLVANIA

9171-A Roosevelt Blvd, Philadelphia,
PA 19114
215-676-9494

SOUTH CAROLINA

243 King Street, Charleston,
SC 29401   843-577-0175

TENNESSEE

4811 Poplar Avenue, Memphis,
TN 38117   901-761-2987

TEXAS

114 Main Plaza, San Antonio,
TX 78205   210-224-8101

VIRGINIA

1025 King Street, Alexandria,
VA 22314   703-549-3806

CANADA

3022 Dufferin Street, Toronto,
ON M6B 3T5   416-781-9131

1155 Yonge Street, Toronto,
ON M4T 1W2   416-934-3440

¡También somos su fuente para libros,